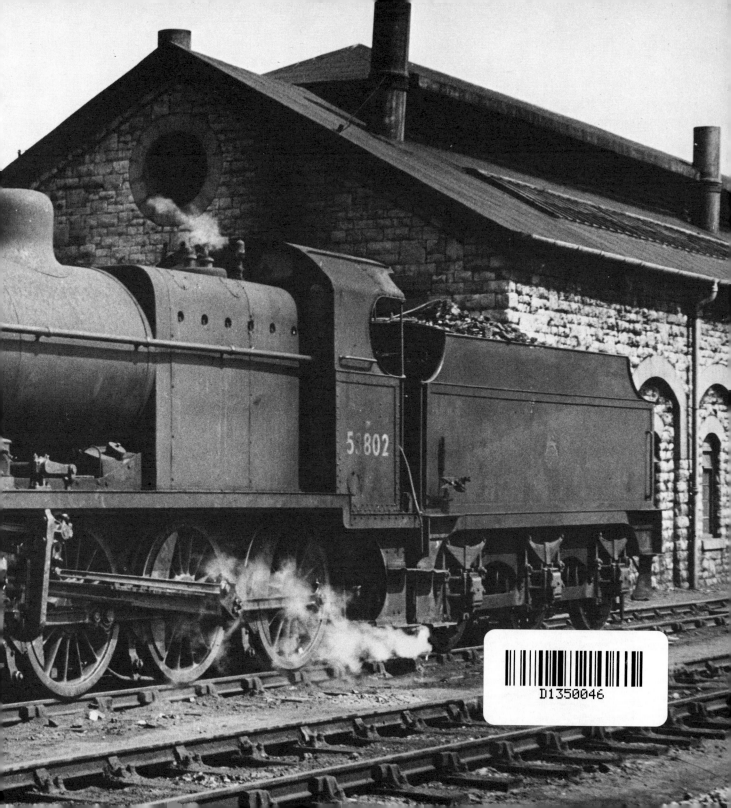

LONDON MIDLAND STEAM locomotives: 1

LONDON MIDLAND STEAM LOCOMOTIVES

A PICTORIAL SURVEY OF EX-LMSR LOCOMOTIVES IN THE 1950s

VOLUME 1

BRIAN MORRISON

D. BRADFORD BARTON LIMITED

Frontispiece: Beyer-Garratt 2-6-0 + 0-6-2T No. 47999 inside Toton shed (18A) in July 1955. A joint Fowler/Beyer Peacock design dating from 1927, this was one of only two of the class that retained the original fixed coal bunker, the remainder having a rotary self-trimming type as illustrated later in this volume.

© copyright D. Bradford Barton Ltd 1975   ISBN 0 85153 199 7

printed in Great Britain by Chapel River Press (IPC Printers), Andover for the publishers

D. BRADFORD BARTON LTD · Trethellan House · Truro · Cornwall · England

introduction

At the grouping of Britain's railways in 1923, the newly formed London Midland & Scottish Railway found itself with over 10,000 steam locomotives of very widely assorted designs, parentage and purpose. At Nationalisation in 1948 the company still had nearly 8,000 but by then there were only something like a 100 different classes left as against the myriad that had existed 25 years earlier. By the early 1950's on the Region, there was still something like 70 different classes remaining and these included not only engines built by the LMS itself but ex-Lancashire & Yorkshire, Caledonian, Highland and Furness types, as well as the obvious ones from the London & North Western and Midland Railways plus their earlier constituent lines such as the North London and London Tilbury & Southend.

Classifying locomotives as 3F, 4P or 5MT, etc. was an ideal arrangement from the operating standpoint but, to other than the specialist, it was often not apparent that Class 3F for example consisted of at least

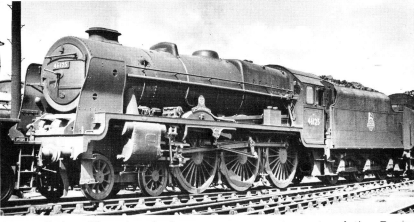

ten entirely different sub-classes which in turn also embraced several variations, of either major or minor importance. The general classification 2P involved some eight different types and even the ubiquitous Class 5MT included three different classes plus many varieties under the one umbrella. This volume, the first of two, illustrates at least one example of each class still working on the London Midland in the 1950's and in addition includes the majority of the varieties. Humbler and less well-known classes as well as those which were confined to working in

more remote parts of the Region have deliberately been given greater prominence than the bigger and more popular wide-ranging or express types which are already adequately recorded elsewhere. On a similar basis, the short selection of locomotive workshop scenes at the conclusion of Volume 2 concentrates elsewhere than the well-known localities of Derby or Crewe. The illustrations are larger than has been seen before in a publication of this type and should appeal to railway modellers and LMS aficionados, plus those who just like to feast their eyes on the locomotive power variety that existed in the final decade of steam on British Railways. The photographs herein were taken in the 1950's before the change to dieselisation and were captured, in the main, whilst on shed. The locations are from as far north as Inverness and as far south as Templecombe—such was the size of the ex-LMSR system. This volume contains the locomotives numbered from 40000 to 47999; the remainder, from 48000 onwards, will be found in Volume 2.

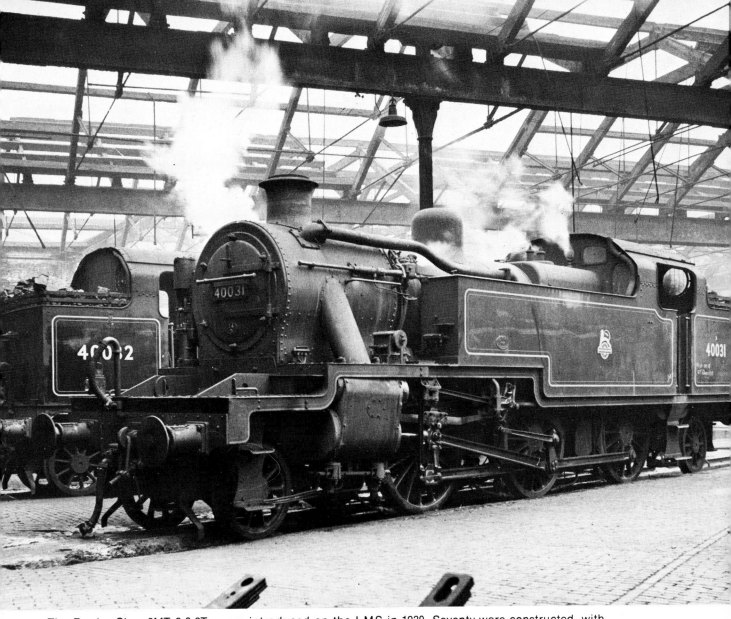

The Fowler Class 3MT 2-6-2Ts were introduced on the LMS in 1930. Seventy were constructed, with parallel boilers and Walschaerts valve gear. With outside cylinders 17½in × 26in. and 5ft 3in driving wheels, they had a tractive effort of 21,485lb. No. 40052 at Trafford Park (9E) in August 1955 has the addition of outside steam pipes, but is otherwise in original condition. No. 40056, fitted for auto working, is at Hull Botanic Gardens (53B) in August 1954 and No. 40031 inside Kentish Town (14B) in December 1954. The latter is fitted with a larger type chimney and condensing apparatus for working through the tunnels of the Metropolitan widened lines.

The Stanier Class 3MT 2-6-2Ts, of which a total of 139 was built, were introduced in 1935 as a development of the Fowler design detailed on the previous page. Having a taper boiler, they were nearly a ton heavier than their counterparts but the design was such as to give them a much smaller appearance. In 1941 four of the class were fitted with larger boilers but any improvement as a result was negligible and the experiment was not continued. The cylinder dimensions, valve gears, size of wheels and tractive effort was identical with the Fowler machines. No. 40127 moves off shed at Liverpool Brunswick (8E), in August 1955, one of the class fitted with a larger diameter chimney. No. 40098, with water feed and steam dome combined, stands in the sunshine of July 1954 in the yards at Shrewsbury (84G), whilst No. 40168, with separate top feed and original style chimney, poses at Bolton (26C) in July 1955.

The Johnson Midland 2P '483' Class 4-4-0s, originally constructed between 1882 and 1901, were rebuilt by Deeley from 1904 onwards and modified again by Fowler between 1912 and 1923 with superheater and piston valves. With 7ft 0½in driving wheels, 20½in × 26in cylinders and a working pressure of 160lb, they produced a tractive effort of 17,585lb. No. 40407, one of the first batch to be built and one of the forerunners of a class that was to number nearly 300, was photographed at Derby (17A) in July 1955. No. 40562, with early style BR lettering, is at Rose Grove (24B), Lancashire. No. 40323, shown inside Leeds Holbeck (20A), was one of four locomotives introduced new in 1914 for the Somerset & Dorset Joint Railway and taken into LMS stock in 1930.

11

The Fowler Class 2P 4-4-0s were built between 1928 and 1932 and these 135 locomotives were the last Midland Railway type to be chosen for construction by the LMS. Having 6ft 9in driving wheels, 19in × 26in cylinders and a working pressure of 180lb, these 54-ton machines had a tractive effort of 17,730lb. No. 40680, with short chimney, is highlighted by the morning sun at Wigan L & Y (27D) in 1955; No. 40634 was one of the two engines built for the Somerset & Dorset.

13

More than half the Fowler 2P 4-4-0s were allocated to Scottish Region and, apart from being in much better external condition generally than those further south, a number retained the original Fowler chimney as seen on No. 40614, at Dumfries (68B) in 1957. No. 40672, appearing to sport a chimney from the Johnson 4-4-0s, waits in the rain at Watford Junction in 1952, whilst No. 40633, photographed inside Burton-on-Trent shed (17B) in 1955, was one of two in the class fitted with Dabeg feed water heater. This was the other locomotive taken into LMS stock from the S & DJR in 1930. Note the much more squat Stanier chimney as compared with No. 40672.

Sir Henry Fowler's Class 4P three-cylinder compound 4-4-0s were introduced in 1924 although he did not actually succeed George Hughes as Chief Mechanical Engineer of the LMSR until a year later. The class eventually totalled 195 engines, the last being built in 1932. Basically the design was an LMS development of the Midland compound, but with 6ft 9in driving wheels and, in most cases, reduced boiler mountings. The outside cylinders measured 21in × 26in and the inside one 19in × 26in. A pressure of 200lb produced a tractive effort of 22,650lb. Here, No. 40907, of Millhouses (19B), lines up alongside sister engine No. 41111 and a Stanier 2-6-4T outside Trafford Park shed in August 1955. One of the Scottish compounds with original type chimney, No. 40939 rests outside Aberdeen Ferryhill (61B) in 1953, having acted as pilot engine for the 'Granite City'. The first batch of 'Compounds' built in 1924 still retained the Midland Railway style right-hand drive despite the fact that the standard driving position for the LMS was on the left! Later they were converted and the left-hand position is clearly shown in this view of No. 41157 outside its home shed at Chester (6A).

17

The Class 2MT 2-6-2Ts were an Ivatt taper boiler design of 1946 intended for branch line work. Construction was continued by BR until 1952 when the very similar Standard 2MT 84000 Class came into being. Nicknamed 'Mickey Mouses' the class numbered 130 and the first 90 had cylinders of 16in × 24in dimension with Walschaerts valve gear and a tractive effort of 17,410lb; the final batch of 40, with 16½in × 24in cylinders, produced 18,510lb. Both types weighed 63¼ tons and had 5ft driving wheels. One of the first batch, No. 41210, fitted for push-and-pull working, is seen at Warrington (8B) in 1955; No. 41304, of the later batch, is sandwiched between GWR locomotives at Swindon in February the same year. Below, one of the locomotives allocated to Southern Region, No. 41300, stands in the evening sunshine at Bricklayers Arms (73B) in September 1954.

Johnson Midland Class OF 0-4-0ST No. 41516, one of a class of 26 locomotives built between 1883 and 1903 for shunting in docks and brewery yards, was still on active service at Burton-on-Trent (17B) in the autumn of 1955. One of the smallest of the numerous LMS tanks, this dainty little engine weighed just over 23 tons and had 3ft 10in driving wheels, 13in × 20in cylinders and a working pressure of 140lb.

A larger version of the type shown opposite, No. 41518 dated from 1897 and, whilst retaining the same wheel diameter and boiler pressure, had larger (15in × 20in) cylinders and a weight of over 32 tons with a tractive effort of 11,640lb compared to 8,745lb of the smaller No. 41516. The photograph was taken at Staveley (18D) in September 1955.

Deeley's Class OF 0-4-0T, constructed between 1907 and 1922, was designed specifically for work on the Midland in places where a short wheel base was necessary to negotiate sharp curves, in docks and other industrial sites. Having outside 15in × 22in cylinders and Walschaerts valve gear, with 3ft 9½in wheels and a pressure of 160lb, they produced a t.e. of 14,635lb and weighed approximately 33 tons. No. 41532 is inside the shed at Burton-on-Trent and No. 41535 inside Derby: 1955.

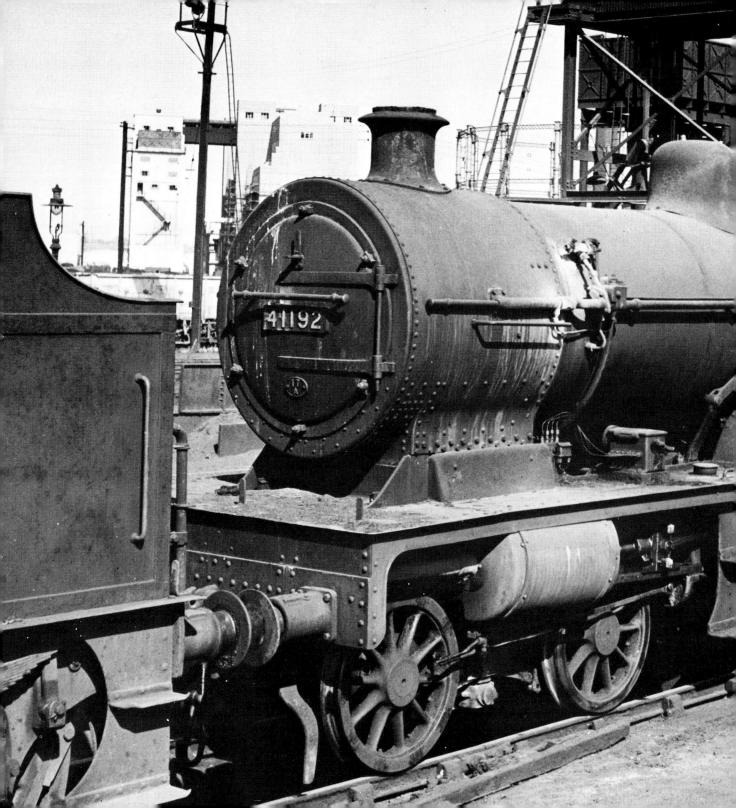

Class 4P 4-4-0
'Compound' No. 41192
outside Derby shed
in July 1954.
Originally known as
the 'Scarlet Runners',
they lost this nickname
soon after losing their
post-1927 crimson
livery and, at least
from Nationalisation,
were usually
referred to merely
as 'Compounds'. The
last of the class was
withdrawn in 1961.

Designed by S. W. Johnson for the Midland Railway and built in 1878–99, nearly 50 Class 1F 0-6-0Ts survived to the middle 1950's, a fine tribute in itself to a sound design. No. 41713 (below), seen inside the shed at Kentish Town (14B), retains the original Johnson boiler and half-section cab. No. 41699 still has the half-section cab but has been rebuilt with a Belpaire boiler, whilst No. 41726 has the same boiler but an all-over cab. These locomotives weighed 39½ tons and with 17in × 24in cylinders and 4ft 7in wheels had a tractive effort of 16,080lb at 150lb pressure for the Johnson boilered engines and 15,005lb at 140lb for the Belpaire-boilered rebuilds. No. 41699, although still carrying a Swansea Victoria shed-plate (87K), was actually photographed at Burton-on-Trent, and No. 41726 was just out of Derby Works, July 1955.

Produced during the initial period of Stanier's reign as CME at Crewe, the Class 2P 0-4-4Ts totalled ten in number and were introduced on the LMS in 1932. All were fitted for auto working, weighing just over 58 tons, with 18in × 26in cylinders and a working pressure of 160lb. 5ft 7in driving wheels gave a useful turn of speed. No. 41908, seen at Longsight shed (9A), at Manchester in August 1955, shows her obvious Midland parentage. All the class had been withdrawn by 1962.

Whitelegg's London, Tilbury & Southend Railway '79' Class 4-4-2Ts were first introduced in 1909 as rebuilds from a smaller class that had initially been built in 1897–98. Three of the class were actually completely new (including No. 41966 seen overleaf) until the period 1923–30 when the LMS revived the design and produced a further 35 locomotives with detail differences. Photographed at Stratford (30A) on 10 April 1954, No. 41952 was one of the last batch and built in 1927.

Last of the original LT & SR '79' Class 4-4-2Ts was No. 41966 of the 1909 batch, seen here at Toton (18A) on 11 September 1955. As with all the class, No. 41966 had 170lb boiler pressure, 19in × 26in outside cylinders, Stephenson valve gear and 6ft 6in driving wheels. Until 1923 the class consisted of sixteen engines, all of which carried place names associated with the line such as *Forest Gate*, *Leytonstone*, *Stratford*, *Shoeburyness* and *Westcliff*. This particular locomotive was numbered 80 and carried the name *Thundersley*. Under the LMS power classification they were rated 3P.

30

Hardly resembling the forlorn machine opposite but, nevertheless, one and the same locomotive, this photograph epitomises what restoration and preservation are all about. To commemorate the centenary of the opening of the line to Southend, *Thundersley* was restored to original London, Tilbury & Southend livery and is here seen outside Stratford Works on 10 March 1956, duly decorated.

Carrying a Southend (Victoria) 30D shedplate, one of the last batch of LT & S R '79' Class 3P 4-4-2Ts No. 41970 at Stratford in April 1954.

Another London, Tilbury & Southend design that lasted well into the post-Nationalisation years was the '69' Class 3F 0-6-2T also introduced by Whitelegg. Built between 1903–12, these 64-ton engines had 5ft 3in driving wheels, 170lb boiler pressure, 18in × 26in cylinders and a tractive effort of 19,320lb. No. 41989 was originally named *Dagenham Dock* and No. 41982 *Wakering*.

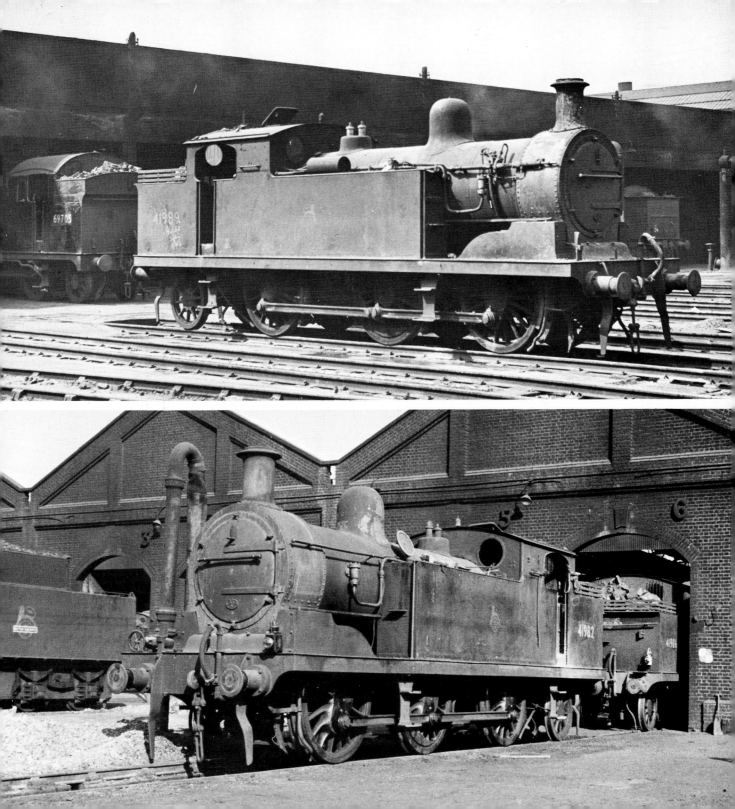

Fairburn's Class 4MT 2-6-4Ts were introduced on the LMS in 1945 and building continued under British Railways until by 1951 the class numbered 277, the final 41 being built at Brighton for use on the Southern Region. Weighing just over 85 tons, these handsome tank locomotives had a boiler pressure of 200lb, outside cylinders of $19\frac{5}{8}$in × 26in and 5ft 9in driving wheels. No. 42059 is at Greenock (Princes Pier) in June 1957; No. 42087 at Stewarts Lane in August 1954, and immaculate No. 42258 at Greenock Ladyburn (66D). Even the hinges on the smoke-box door have been painted silver by the staff at No. 42258's home shed.

Fowler's Class 4MT 2-6-4Ts were built between 1927 and 1934, totalling 125 locomotives. Apart from being rebuilt with outside steam pipes and having the trailing bogie brakes removed, the class ran unchanged throughout their life of 40 years or so. No. 42367, having the firebox cleaned out at Longsight in the midsummer of 1955, was withdrawn in 1962, 37 of the class being withdrawn in that year.

Another Fowler Class 4MT 2-6-4T, No. 42390, amid the clutter outside Shrewsbury shed (84G) in July 1954, awaiting a return duty to Chester. Weighing $86\frac{1}{4}$ tons with 19in × 26in cylinders, 5ft 9in driving wheels and a boiler pressure of 200lb, the class produced a tractive effort of 23,125lb.

The last 41 locomotives of Fowler's extremely successful 2-6-4T design differed from the main batch in so far as they were provided with re-designed cabs with side windows; No. 42397 of this type is at Longsight (9A) alongside a Stanier Class 8F and a 'Jubilee'.

Stanier's contribution to the already extensive LMS stud of 2-6-4Ts was introduced in 1935 and construction continued until 1943 when the fleet then numbered 206. With outside cylinders, Walschaerts valve gear and taper boiler, the Stanier versions weighed 3cwt short of 88 tons, had 19½in × 26in cylinders, 200lb boiler pressure, and a tractive effort of 24,670lb. As with the Fowlers, driving wheel diameter was 5ft 9in and the class continued to give service every bit as useful and troublefree as these earlier engines. No. 42469 was one of them allocated to Trafford Park; No. 42426 (below) at Liverpool, Edge Hill (8A) is occupied shunting the Widnes staff coach.

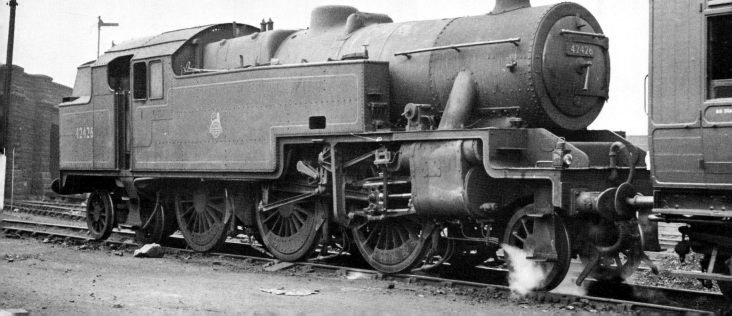

An unusual view at Camden (1B) shed on a Sunday morning in July 1958. On the turntable is unrebuilt 'Patriot' Class No. 45546 *Fleetwood*, from Crewe North (5A); in the background, ready for the day's duties, are a Caprotti 'Black Five', a rebuilt 'Patriot', a 'Duchess' and another 'Black Five'.

Stanier's 3-cylinder version of the 2-6-4T numbered only 47 and for most of their life were allocated to the ex-LT & S sheds at Plaistow (33A) and Shoeburyness (33C). It was found that the design, introduced in 1934, showed no particular superiority over the older Fowler engines and Stanier reverted to a 2-cylinder layout from 1935. The 3-cylinder locomotives could be distinguished externally by the integrated steam dome and water feed as well as the longer outside steam pipes. No. 42525 outside Plaistow shed in April 1955 is a typical example of the class, which differed from their sister engines by having a weight of $92\frac{1}{4}$ tons, 16in × 26in cylinders and a 24,600lb tractive effort.

The Stanier 2-cylinder Class 4MT 2-6-4Ts were to be found throughout the length and breadth of the Midland Region, popular everywhere with the enginemen and shed staff. No. 42557 is shown in 'ex works' condition outside Newton Heath (26A) whilst No. 42628 stands outside what remained of the Brunswick (8E) depot at Liverpool which was never repaired following wartime bomb damage.

Built from 1926 to 1932, the Hughes Class 5MT 2-6-0 was the first completely new design of locomotive to appear on the LMS. Known originally as the 'Horwich Moguls' after their place of birth, they eventually received the nickname 'Crabs' in view of the appearance given by their big inclined cylinders and raised running plate over these. Very capable and well-liked engines capable of a wide range of mixed traffic duties, they weighed 66 tons, with 21in × 26in cylinders, 180lb boiler pressure, and 5ft 6in driving wheels giving a tractive effort of 26,580lb. No. 42837 is seen at Glasgow St. Rollox (65B) on 23 June 1957 and No. 42812 at Willesden (1A) on 20 March 1955. Both are in the lined black BR livery of the mid-1950's.

45

Although designed by George Hughes, the 'Crabs' did not actually appear in service on the LMS until after his retirement and, in consequence, the class had a number of fittings that were pure Fowler, particularly the tender. In 1931 five of this class of 245 engines were experimentally fitted with Lentz rotary-cam poppet valve gear in place of the standard Walschaerts type. This was, in turn, replaced with Reidinger poppet valve gear in 1953. The standard Walschaerts valve gear of No. 42727 at Manchester, Newton Heath (26A), in 1955 can be compared with the Reidinger variety, shown in close-up on No. 42822 at Burton-on-Trent shortly after conversion in 1954.

Stanier's development of the Class 5MT 2-6-0 appeared in 1933 and by the following year 40 of them had been put into service. Built with a taper boiler, pressed to 225lb, they weighed 69 tons 2cwt, had 5ft 6in driving wheels and a t.e. of 26,290lb. The two outside cylinders, positioned horizontally it will be noticed, were 18in × 28in. No. 42970 was recorded outside Birkenhead (6C) on a winter day in 1956; and No. 42948 at Willesden (1A) in March of the previous year. The class were withdrawn 1963–66.

Ivatt's up-dated design for a mixed-traffic mogul appeared in 1947 but only the first three engines were turned out by the LMS in December of that year, the remaining 159 being built under the auspices of BR in 1948–52. The earlier locomotives had a double chimney but, following experiments with a single blast pipe and chimney on No. 43027, the remainder of the class from No. 43050 on appeared with the latter and the original 50 were duly altered. The keynote of Ivatt's design was simplicity and accessibility, with exposed piping, high running boards, plus angular tender and cab. No. 43001 as originally built by the LMS and still retaining the double chimney, rests outside Devons Road (1D) shed in London in the spring of 1955. No. 43024, as rebuilt with single chimney and blastpipe, is seen at the same location in August 1957; No. 43058 of the last batch (with tablet catcher inset into the tender side) is at Stratford after works overhaul there in August 1954.

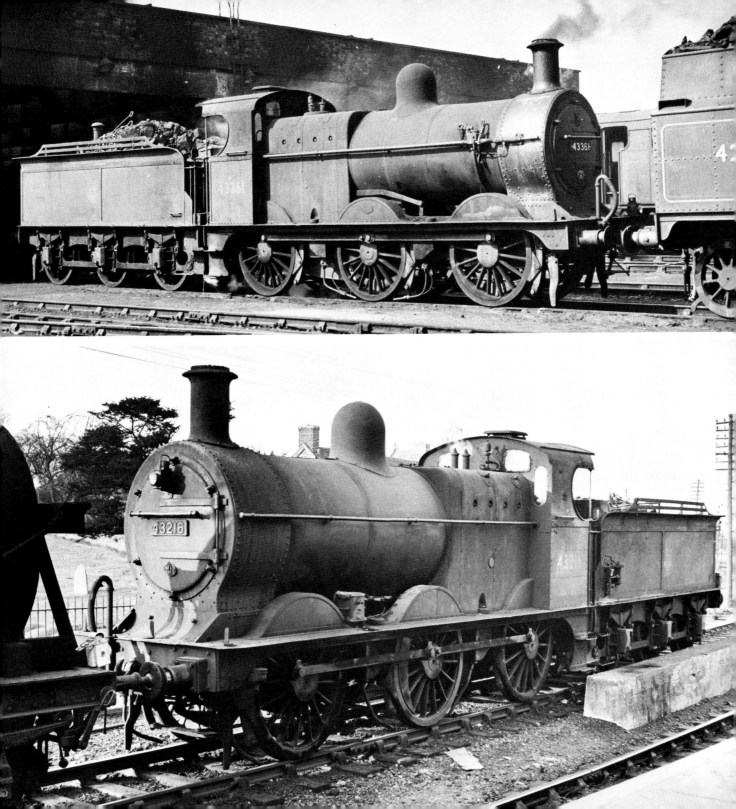

The numerous Midland Railway Class 3F 0-6-0s first appeared in 1885 and were rebuilt from 1916 by Fowler with Belpaire boilers. Weighing 44 tons, these rebuilt engines had a boiler pressure of 175lb and 18in × 26in cylinders. Those with 4ft 11in driving wheels had a tractive effort of 21,240lb whilst the majority, with 5ft 3in wheels, were rated at 19,890lb. No. 43341 at Sheffield (19A), August 1955; No. 43361 at Stafford (5C), in August 1956; and No. 43216 at Templecombe in Somerset, April 1956. Note the tablet exchange apparatus fitted to the tender of the latter, one of the locomotives built for the Somerset & Dorset in 1896 and subsequently taken into LMS stock.

53

Deeley's Class 3F 0-6-0s dated from 1906, a continuation of the original Johnson design for the Midland Railway, described on the previous page. They were similarly rebuilt in the Fowler era, with Belpaire boiler and, although having the same cylinders and valve gear, were somewhat heavier at 46 tons 3cwt, and had a tractive effort of 21,010lb. All the class had 5ft 3in driving wheels. No. 43822 was photographed on Shrewsbury shed in July 1954.

In 1911 Fowler introduced his Class 4F 0-6-0s which were superheated with a boiler pressure of 175lb, weighed 48¾ tons and had 20in × 26in cylinders and a tractive effort of 24,555lb. Again they retained 5ft 3in wheels and Stephenson valve gear. No. 43964 in the class is seen receiving attention at Kentish Town (14B) in June 1955; No. 43998 shortly after 'shopping' at Derby in July of the same year.

54

Fowler Class 4F
No. 44257 outside
Perth (63A) shed in
July 1957. This was
one of the final
development of the
six-coupled freight
design started by
Johnson in 1885,
introduced to the
LMS in 1924 and
built from then up to
the early 1940's.

The last batch of 4Fs were naturally of slightly larger dimensions and a more sophisticated design than the original type but could still clearly claim the ancestry of the 1885 engines. With 43 from the Somerset & Dorset and sixteen from the Midland & Great Northern, the number built was a remarkable 1,761, a total that must constitute a record for this country. No. 44412 from Nottingham (16A), having been through Bow Works, is in immaculate condition at Devons Road Depot in March 1957. A later type chimney is evident than the one fitted to No. 44257 on the previous page.

Ex S & DJR Class 4F No. 44558, with tablet exchanger fitted to the tender, at Bath on 21 April 1956. As with the remainder of this very numerous class, all the 4Fs had the same specifications as described on page 54.

The Stanier Class 5MT two-cylinder 4-6-0s became known everywhere as the 'Black Fives' and between 1934 and 1951 a total of no less than 842 of these superb mixed traffic machines were constructed by the LMS and by BR. The standard engines weighed 72 tons 2cwt, had $18\frac{1}{2}$in × 28in cylinders and Walschaerts valve gear. The taper boiler had a pressure of 225lb, the driving wheels were of 6ft diameter and the tractive effort was 25,455lb. No. 44684, which entered service in 1950, was one of a batch fitted with Skefco roller bearings and with the top feed placed on the first boiler ring. The weight of this particular type of engine was 75 tons 6cwt. Photographed at Crewe North (5A) in August 1955.

No. 44669 was one of the many Scottish-based 'Black Fives' and this example was also introduced in 1950 but unlike No. 44684 had roller bearings on the driving coupled axle only and with top feed closer to the steam dome. Photographed at Carlisle Kingmoor (68A), in June 1957.

Three further varieties of Stanier Class 5s. No. 44727 was introduced in 1949, being one of those with a steel firebox, and is seen at St. Rollox (65B) in June 1957. No. 44688, fitted with Timken roller bearings on the driving coupled axle, was put into service in 1950 and is seen at its home depot of Bank Hall (27A). The most distinctive of all the experimental types were those fitted with Caprotti valve gear. No. 44752, from Longsight, was also fitted with Timken roller bearings and stands over the pits at Camden Town (1B) in July 1958. These Caprotti engines entered service in 1948 and had an increased weight over the standard variety of approximately two tons.

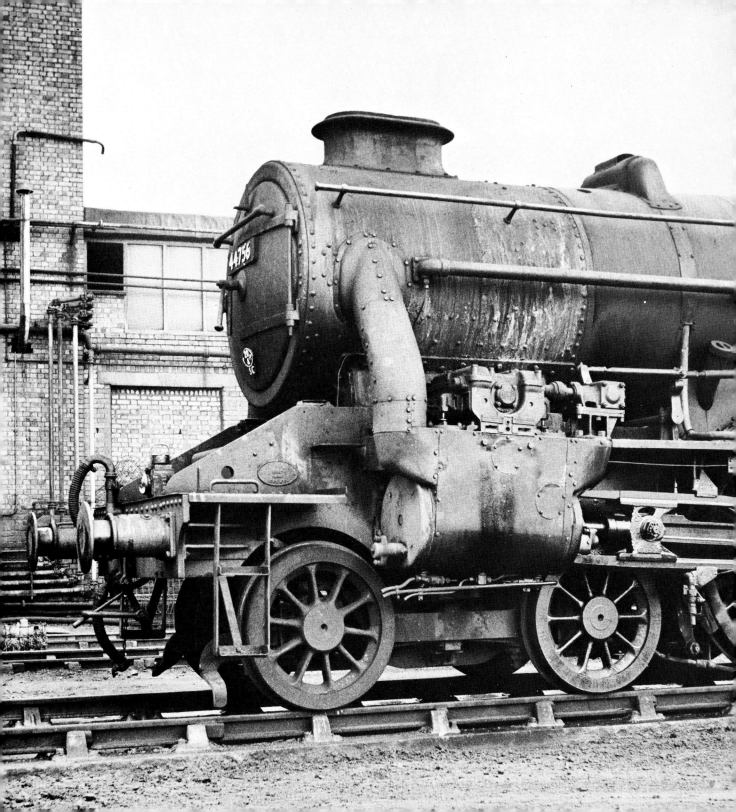

Another variety of the Caprotti Class 5MT 4-6-0s were three engines introduced in 1948 with Timken roller bearings and—much more obvious—double chimneys. This trio were allocated to Leeds Holbeck (20A) including No. 44755 and No. 44756 photographed at Kentish Town and Wakefield respectively.

Introduced in 1930, the first two of the Fowler 'Patriot' Class 6P 4-6-0s were rebuilds of the LNWR 'Claughtons' retaining, among other details, the original wheels distinguished by the large centre bosses. These latter are apparent in the illustration (left) of No. 45501 *St. Dunstan's* on the turntable at Shrewsbury in July 1954. The small, unusual nameplate device was also a minor distinguishing feature on this, the second of the 'Patriots'. No. 45501 (originally No. 5902 when turned out from Derby in 1930), was withdrawn in 1961.

No. 45506 *The Royal Pioneer Corps* was one of the locomotives that were officially regarded as 'Claughton' rebuilds but, in fact, were entirely new, being turned out from Crewe in 1932. This scene is at Carlisle Upperby in June 1957. Withdrawal of the 'Patriots' came from 1960–65.

Another 'Patriot', No. 45518 *Bradshaw*, ready for the road outside Edge Hill shed at Liverpool on 22 August 1955. The class were popular with footplate crews and operating authorities alike, at home on fast freights and heavy secondary express work. Although about five tons lighter than their bigger sisters the 'Royal Scots', driven hard they could give almost as good an account of themselves as the latter before the era of rebuilding.

Of the 52 'Patriots' only eight were never named. One of these, No. 45508, ran for some time with a most unpleasant-looking thin stovepipe chimney as seen here at Carlisle Upperby in 1957. This was a product of draughting experiments carried out with this member of the class a decade or so earlier. These locomotives were originally nicknamed 'Baby Scots' but the name *Patriot* was transferred from a withdrawn 'Claughton' and they were officially given this as the title for the class.

From 1946 onwards, H. G. Ivatt commenced rebuilding the 'Patriots' which, like the Royal Scots, were beginning to show serious signs of wear in their vitals, and eventually seventeen were to emerge with larger taper boilers pressed to 250lb, new 17in × 26in cylinders and double chimneys. Classified as 7P, in this form, they had a tractive effort of 29,570lb. No. 45512 *Bunsen* at Camden Town on 6 July 1958, No. 45529 *Stephenson* and No. 45523 *Bangor*, both photographed at Carlisle Upperby on 28 June 1957, show how very little remained unchanged in this radical rebuild.

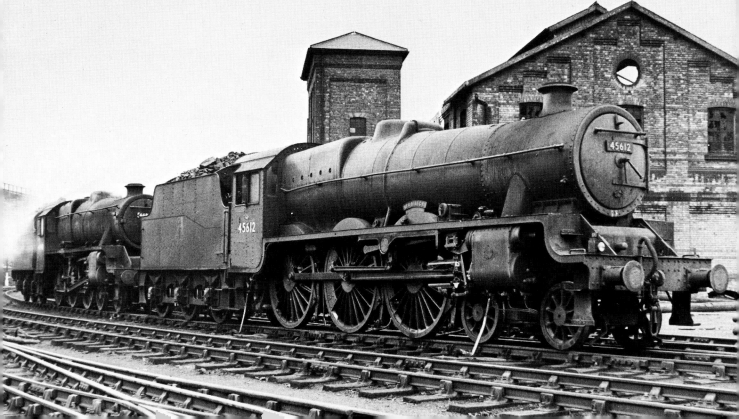

The 'Jubilee' Class 6P (originally 5XP) were basically Stanier's taper-boilered development of the 'Patriots' and between 1934–36 a total of 191 of these three cylinder 4-6-0s was built. Weighing just under 80 tons, their boiler pressure was 225lb, cylinders 17in × 26in, driving wheels 6ft 9in and tractive effort 26,610lb. No. 45552 *Silver Jubilee* (at Stafford in August 1956), with raised numerals on the cab side, has the standard self-trimming Stanier tender; No. 45612 *Jamaica* (at Nottingham shed in 1955) has the earlier type of Stanier flat-sided tender as fitted to ten of the class; No. 45591 *Udiapur*, at Shrewsbury (84G) in July 1954, has the small 3,500 gallon Fowler tender carried by a few of the Jubilees.

73

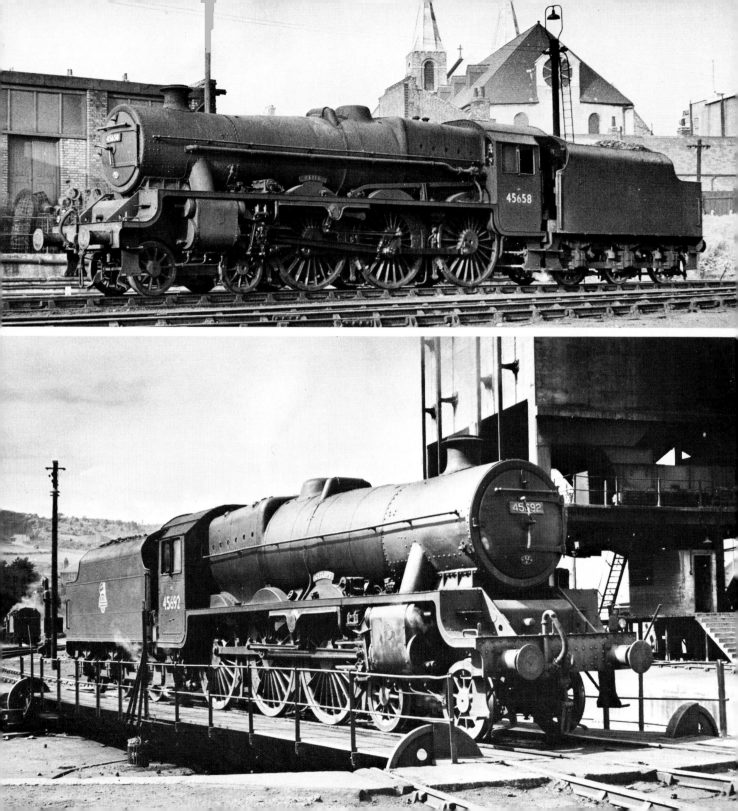

The 'Jubilees' were to be seen nearly everywhere on London Midland Region and some 24 were allocated to Scottish Region sheds. One of these, No. 45692 *Cyclops*, in the excellent condition usual north of the border, stands on the turntable at Perth (63A) in June 1957. No. 45658 *Keyes*, at Kentish Town (14B) in June 1955, was one of the class regularly seen on the Midland route out of St. Pancras, for long a preserve of the 'Jubilees'.

In 1942 No. 45735 *Comet* and No. 45736 *Phoenix* were rebuilt with a larger boiler and double chimney in similar style to the 'Patriots' and 'Royal Scots'. New larger diameter boilers, double chimneys and the addition of smoke deflectors at a later date, altered the appearance of this pair radically from that of the original class. No. 45736, photographed on a parcels train at Stafford in 1956, was withdrawn in 1964, along with No. 45735.

46163

46106

4610

The 'Royal Scot' class, introduced by Fowler in 1927, were all rebuilt as they became due for heavy repair between 1943 and 1955 under a modernisation programme instituted by Sir William Stanier. The original parallel boilers were replaced with the taper variety and they also received new cylinders and a double chimney. Weighing 83 tons they had a boiler pressure of 250lb, 18in × 26in cylinders with Walschaerts valve gear, 6ft 9in driving wheels and a tractive effort of 33,150lb. The class totalled 70 plus the rebuilt high pressure locomotive *Fury* which, after rebuild, could not be distinguished from the remainder of the class (although it was, in fact, a ton heavier). No. 46163 *Civil Service Rifleman* at Manchester Newton Heath (26A) in 1955; No. 46140 *The King's Royal Rifle Corps*, with later style B R crest on the tender, on the turntable at Camden Town in 1959; No. 46106 *Gordon Highlander*, fitted with B R type smoke deflectors, at Crewe North (5A) in 1958.

77

The first of Stanier's locomotives to appear on the LMS after his appointment as Chief Mechanical Engineer in 1932 was the magnificent 'Princess Royal' class Pacific which emerged from Crewe Works in July 1933. Weighing 104½ tons and having a tractive effort of 40,285lb, they were fitted with a 250lb superheated taper boiler and four 16¼in × 28in cylinders with Walschaerts valve gear and 6ft 6in driving wheels. Twelve were constructed by 1935 plus the ill-fated 'Turbomotive' that was destroyed, soon after having been rebuilt, in the Harrow & Wealdstone disaster. Stanier then turned his attention to the heavier 'Coronation' class Pacifics which were, in effect, a development of the 'Princess Royals'. No. 46200 *The Princess Royal,* immaculate in red livery in July 1958, only just fits onto the Camden turntable; No. 46206 *Princess Marie Louise,* (of the second batch built in 1935 with modified valve gear, boiler and detail differences) newly painted in Brunswick green livery, awaits the next duty turn at Glasgow Polmadie (66A) in June 1957; No. 46201 *Princess Elizabeth* in fog-shrouded Camden Town depot in December 1954. Withdrawal of the class commenced in 1961 but fortunately two of these fine Pacifics have been preserved.

Stanier's 'Coronation' Class 8P Pacifics, constructed between 1938 and 1948, were described as an 'enlargement' of the 'Princess Royals' although their tractive effort was slightly less at 40,000lb. The driving wheels were, however, three inches larger in diameter at 6ft 9in and their weight was a formidable 105¼ tons. Cylinders and boiler pressure were the same. 38 locomotives made up the class, 24 of these being originally streamlined but the casings were removed between 1946 and 1949. The last two of the class were an Ivatt development of the original 36, having roller bearings and some detail differences. No. 46232 *Duchess of Montrose* inside Crewe North (5A) shed in 1955 was one of the non-streamlined series of pre-war build. No. 46255 *City of Hereford* at Camden Town in 1958 appeared from Crewe works in 1946 and shows detail differences from the earlier ones. The figure of the fireman shows well the size of these fine locomotives which were responsible for working the heaviest Anglo-Scottish expresses from the late 1930s until the end of steam. Overleaf, No. 46234 *Duchess of Abercorn*, built in 1938 as one of the first non-streamlined batch of five, seen at Crewe North in 1955.

The Webb LNWR Class 1P 2-4-2Ts were introduced in 1890 and 160 were constructed in the following eight years, for light branch-line passenger work. The first was withdrawn in 1921 but 43 of the class survived to Nationalisation and the last was not withdrawn until 1955. Weighing some 50 tons, with 5ft 6in driving wheels and a boiler pressure of 150lb, they had a tractive effort of 12,910lb. The inside cylinders were 17in × 24in and they had Joy valve gear. Photographed at Warwick (2C) in July 1954, shortly before being scrapped, No. 46712 was engaged in working the Coventry–Leamington Spa auto train and is seen here being coaled up between turns.

Ivatt's Class 2MT Moguls were light locomotives—weight 47 tons—that were introduced by the LMS two years before Nationalisation. BR continued the building programme until 1952 when the class (then numbering 128) was superseded by the almost identical BR Standard design numbered in the 78000 series. These Ivatt engines were more or less a tender version of the Ivatt Class 2MT 2-6-2Ts described on page 18 and had the same 200lb boiler pressure, 16in × 24in cylinders and a tractive effort of 17,410lb. No. 46455, with wide chimney, at Workington (12D) in June 1957; No. 46489, with taller narrow chimney, also at Workington, was one of the last batch of 63 engines with 16½in × 24in cylinders and slightly increased tractive effort; No. 46511 also of the later batch, at Oswestry in July 1954, fitted with wide chimney.

Class OF 0-4-0ST No. 47001 at Liverpool Bank Hall (27A) shed in 1955. Not built until the early 1950's this was one of the last new engines of basically LMS design to be constructed and the last four of these small shunters remained in service until as late in the diesel era as 1966. Built by Kitsons of Leeds to Stanier's specifications in 1932, these diminutive locomotives were intended for dock shunting and colliery lines etc. where severe curves were found. Five were constructed in this first batch, weighing 33 tons in working order and with a tractive effort of 14,205lb; wheels were 3ft 10in diameter, cylinders $15\frac{1}{2}$in $\times$ 30in and boiler pressure 160lb.

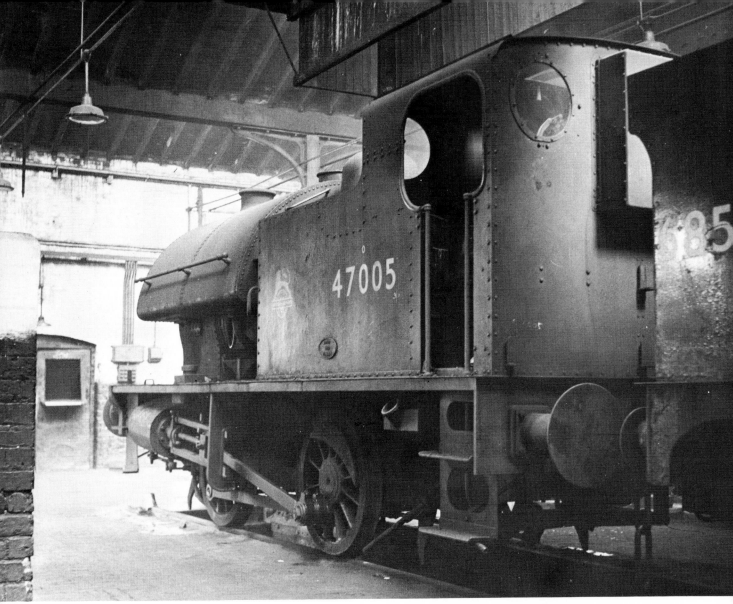

Twenty-one years later another five Class OF saddletanks were built at Horwich Works with shortened saddletanks, the last to be numbered in the 40000 series. These were a ton heavier than the first series and had provision for coal ahead of the footplate to avoid the practice of piling it along the running plate as shown opposite. No. 47005 of this series is shown inside Birkenhead shed where she was stationed for dock use.

The bigger Fowler Class 2F six-coupled tanks were also designed with a short wheelbase for dock working and were built in 1928. These ten engines (Nos. 47160–69) weighed 43 tons 12cwt and had a boiler pressure of 160lb, with outside 17in × 22in cylinders and Walschaerts valve gear. The wheels were 3ft 11in in diameter and tractive effort 18,400lb. Nos. 47164 and 47166 were both photographed at Bidston (6F) in 1955. The last three of the class were scrapped in 1963, including No. 47166—alas before the era of widespread preservation of locomotives, as these handy little tanks would have been ideal subjects for this.

The Johnson Midland Class 3F 0-6-0Ts were built between 1899 and 1902, totalling 60 locomotives. All were rebuilt with Belpaire boilers from 1919 onwards and these engines were the forerunners of the famous so-called 'Jinties' which came upon the scene in 1924. Weighing just under 49 tons, they had a boiler pressure of 160lb, 4ft 7in wheels, 18in × 26in cylinders and a tractive effort of 20,835lb. Nos. 47220 and 47224 (left) were both fitted with condensing apparatus for working through the Metropolitan line tunnels in London and are seen at Cricklewood (14A) shed in November 1954. More typical was No. 47250 (above), one of the class built without condensers, at Derby (17A) in 1955.

The 'Jinty' Class 3F 0-6-0Ts were a development of the Midland engines described on page 91, the 422 locomotives in this class being regarded as the standard LMS shunter. In design and appearance they were almost the same as the earlier type but had extended smoke boxes and lower tanks without the shaping at the cab door. Built in batches from 1924–30, all except the last five (which were Horwich-built), were constructed by outside builders (Vulcan Foundry, Hunslet, North British, Bagnall, Beardmore). By 1964 only 146 remained in service, and 83 by 1965, the last four surviving to the main withdrawal of 1967, Nos. 47314 and 47315 (left) were two of the class built for use on the Somerset & Dorset. No. 47315, it will be noted, has the older type of steam dome as fitted to the Johnson engines. No. 47483, also photographed at Devons Road shed, is a standard member of the class.

Webb's LNWR Class 1F 0-4-2ST constructed between 1896 and 1901 originally totalled twenty in number. At first classified 1P, they could hardly have been intended for passenger duties as they were not fitted with vacuum brakes and the correct 1F title was given in 1927 when they were renumbered into the LMS freight grouping number classifications. Two of the class survived to receive a BR number and one of these, No. 47862, was on duty as Crewe Works shunter in August 1954. Weight was 34 tons 17cwt and with 4ft 5½in driving wheels, a 150lb boiler pressure and 17in × 24in cylinders, they had a nominal tractive effort of 16,530lb.

The jointly developed Fowler and Beyer Peacock 'Beyer-Garratt' 2-6-0 + 0-6-2Ts were built by the latter company between 1927 and 1930, having been designed to handle heavy freight working, particularly the Toton to Brent coal traffic. Front and rear views of the type with the rotary self-trimming coal bunker are shown above, and may be compared with the Frontispiece showing one of the class with the fixed type bunker. Nos. 47991 and 47971 are shown at Cricklewood (14A) and Toton (18A) respectively in 1954.

A close-up of the Walschaerts valve gear of Beyer-Garratt No. 47991. The locomotive weighed 155½ tons as compared to the 148 tons-odd of the type with a fixed bunker. All 33 built had boiler pressure of 190lb, 18½in × 26in cylinders, driving wheels 5ft 3in in diameter, and a tractive effort of 45,620lb—the highest of any locomotive on the LMSR even including the Lickey 0-10-0. However the design was not a very successful one, having inadequate bearing surfaces on the coupled wheels which rendered them rather troublesome in service.